Basic Faster Reading
―New Edition―

速読の基礎演習
―最新版―

Casey Malarcher

原　田　慎　一

photographs by	写真・資料提供
Jiji Press Photo	時事通信フォト

音声ファイルのダウンロード/ストリーミング

CD マーク表示がある箇所は、音声を弊社 HP より無料でダウンロード/ストリーミングすることができます。トップページのバナーをクリックし、書籍検索してください。書籍詳細ページに音声ダウンロードアイコンがございますのでそちらから自習用音声としてご活用ください。

https://www.seibido.co.jp

ALL RIGHTS RESERVED The Japanese edition Copyright © 2014 by Seibido Publishing Co., Ltd.

The original text © 2012 was published by Cengage Learning Asia Pte Ltd.

No part of this work covered by the copyright hereon may be reproduced or used in any form or by any means—graphic, electronic or mechanical, including photocopying, recording, taping, web distribution or information storage and retrieval systems—without the written permission of the publisher.

本書の狙い

　本書は，好評を頂いた『速読の基礎演習』*Basic Faster Reading*（Casey Malarcher，森田　彰，原田　慎一）の最新版です．電子書籍・コンピューター問題・女子相撲などの最近の話題を取り入れ，より興味深い内容にいたしました．

　基本語彙で書かれたやさしい英文を読み，内容理解やリスニングの問題を解きながらリーディング力や語彙力を養成できるよう編集された総合教材です．問題の難易度を抑えていますので，英語を苦手とする方に適しています．passageのジャンルは多岐にわたっており，楽しみながら読み進めることができる内容になっています．

　本書は，1課4ページで計20課の構成になっています．1ページ目では，日本語の導入による内容スキーマ（背景知識）の構築と，重要語の意味の確認を行います．この2つのアクティビティにより，本文の内容理解が容易になります．2ページ目で200語程度のpassageを読みます．最新版から重要語や注の語句は太字に変更し，本文のどこで使われているのかが，一目瞭然となっています．3ページ目には，内容理解の問題と要約のリスニング問題があります．内容理解問題は，4択のやさしい問題ですが，本文をきちんと理解していないと間違えてしまう適度な難易度になっています．リスニングはやや難易度が上がりますが，本文と照らし合わせながら聴くとよいと思います．最後の4ページ目で，重要語句の再確認を行い，定着を図ります．

　速読力を鍛えるために，各passageの語数を読み終えた時間で割り，1分間当たりに読むことができる語数 Word Per Minute（WPM）を算出するのも効果的です．1課から20課までのWPMを記録し，速読力の伸長度を可視化するとモチベーションが高まると思います．

　本書は速読テキストですが，文の構造を把握しながら読む精読にも適しています．英文は平易に書かれていますが，関係詞・不定詞・動名詞・分詞などさまざまな文法項目を含んでいます．速読しようとするとpassageの理解がおろそかになるという人は，英文を正確に読むことを優先しましょう．精読の力がつけば，読む速度も自然と速くなります．

　本書の20課を読み終えれば，まとまった英語の文章を読みこなす自信がつくはずです．本書の使い方を良く読んで，楽しみながら学習してください．

　最後に，本書の編集・出版に際して，有益なご助言と多大なご尽力を賜った（株）成美堂の菅野英一氏に心より感謝申し上げます．

2014年7月

編著者

本書の使い方

BEFORE YOU READ
　最初に，本文の内容理解を助ける日本語の簡単な導入があります．導入は本文を読むときのヒントになっています．写真を見ながら，どんな内容が書いてあるのか予測してみてください．

TARGET VOCABULARY
　本文を読む前に，本文で使用されている重要語の意味を確認します．まず，日本語で意味を書いてみて，自信のない単語や知らない単語は辞書で調べてみましょう．次に，それらの定義や同義語がやさしい英語で書かれていますから，それを結びつけて，語句のイメージも定着させてみましょう．

READING PASSAGE
　本文は比較的やさしい単語を使って書かれた200語程度の英文です．自分のレベルに合わせて，読み方を変えるといいでしょう．本文をやさしいと思う人は，時間を計りながら全体の内容を短時間で読み取る速読をしてみましょう．その際にはわからない単語があっても辞書を引かずに，全体の流れから意味を類推しながら読み進めましょう．本文の最後に単語数があります．読み終えたら，単語数を読むのにかかった時間で割ります．例えば，200語の文を4分で読み終えた場合，200語÷4分＝分速50語です．毎回，分速を記録しておけば，速読力の伸びがわかります．本文を難しいと思う人は，冒頭の語彙問題や注の説明に加え，必要に応じて辞書を使うといいでしょう．1文1文時間をかけ，最終的に話の内容が理解できたときの喜びは非常に大きいと思います．本書を終えた後は，以前よりもリーディング力や語彙力が身につき，英語を読むことが楽しくなっているはずです．

READING COMPREHENSION
　リーディング後に本文をきちんと理解していたかどうかを5問の選択問題で確認します．全体的な内容を問う問題もあれば，詳細な内容を問う問題もあります．本文に書かれていないものを選択させるNOT問題は要注意です．自信がない場合は，本文に戻って，解答の根拠となる箇所を探しましょう．

LISTENING COMPREHENSION
　本文の内容の要約をリスニングし，空所に語句を入れ，要約を完成させます．少し難易度が高いアクティビティです．音声を聞いてもわからない場合や，語句が聞き取れてもスペルがわからない場合は，本文を読み返して確認してみましょう．完成した要約を何度も音読し暗記すれば，英語で短い話をするスピーキング力が身につきます．

VOCABULARY REINFORCEMENT
　本文で出てきた重要語句の使い方を選択問題で確認します．問題の形式は，文脈に当てはまる語句を空所に入れるものと，イタリック体の語句の同義語を選ぶものがあります．例文と一緒に覚え，スピーキングやライティングに使えるようにするといい

でしょう．

IDIOMS

本文で使われたイディオムのうち，特に使用頻度が高く，重要と思われる3つのイディオムをピックアップしています．例文を和訳し，その意味を文の中で確認してください．

CONTENTS

Unit 1 **Lions** 1
(百獣の王ライオン)

Unit 2 **Ramen** 5
(ラーメン)

Unit 3 **The Leaning Tower** 9
(ピサの斜塔)

Unit 4 **A Smart Dog** 13
(賢いワンちゃん)

Unit 5 **Twenty-First Century Books** 17
(電子書籍)

Unit 6 **Valentine's Day** 21
(バレンタイン・デー)

Unit 7 **The Taj Mahal** 25
(ある愛の形)

Unit 8 **A Computer Problem** 29
(コンピューターのホットな問題)

Unit 9 **The Mobius Band** 33
(不思議な輪)

Unit 10 **A Long Weekend** 37
(休日の落とし穴)

Unit 11	**Breakfast in America** 41
	（アメリカの朝食）

Unit 12	**The World Cup** 45
	（ワールドカップ）

Unit 13	**Blood Types** 49
	（血液型で性格判断）

Unit 14	**Reality TV** 53
	（リアリティー番組）

Unit 15	**Rodeos** 57
	（ロデオ）

Unit 16	**Women's Sumo** 61
	（女子相撲）

Unit 17	**Studying Abroad** 65
	（海外で学ぼう）

Unit 18	**The Palace of Salt** 69
	（しょっぱいホテル）

Unit 19	**The Mona Lisa** 73
	（モナリザの微笑）

Unit 20	**Lizards** 77
	（トカゲは好きですか）

Word Per Minute 記録シート 81

LIONS

百獣の王ライオン

　百獣の王と呼ばれているライオンですが，どのような特徴を持っているか知っていますか？　その大きな体は何kgぐらいあるのでしょうか？　普段どのようなものを食べ，またどれくらいの量を食べるのでしょうか？　もしライオンが人を襲えば，大変なことになってしまいます．今回はそんなライオンの生態について読んでみましょう．

TARGET VOCABULARY

Look up each word in a dictionary and match it with the closest meaning.

1. bite　　＿＿＿＿＿（　）a. boy or man
2. collar　　＿＿＿＿＿（　）b. girl or woman
3. female　＿＿＿＿＿（　）c. a place where people can see wild animals
4. male　　＿＿＿＿＿（　）d. the part of a shirt or dress which is around the neck
5. zoo　　＿＿＿＿＿（　）e. use teeth to cut or break something

READING PASSAGE

1   Lions have been called the kings of the animal world. These animals can be found **wild** in Africa and India. Lions in Africa can go without water for up to one month, so they have no trouble **during dry times**.

   Without question, lions are also one of the most popular animals to see in **zoos**.
5 Almost every zoo around the world has a few lions.

   It is very easy for people to tell **male** and **female** lions apart. Lions are the only kind of cat that shows this big difference between males and females. A male lion has a **mane**, a large **collar** of hair around the lion's face. Females do not have manes.

10 Male lions are also larger than females. A male lion usually weighs about 200 kilograms.

   Both male and female lions have very strong mouths. They can break the **backs** of other animals with one **bite**. One lion will usually kill between ten and twenty large animals each year for food.

15 It is unusual for lions to kill people. However, in 1898 two lions killed and ate over one hundred people in Kenya before they were shot by a British colonel named P. J. Patterson. This story became the subject of a Hollywood movie called *The Ghost and the Darkness*.

213 words

Notes

wild「野生の」 during dry times「乾季の間」 mane「(ライオンや馬などの) たてがみ」 back「背骨」「背中」 The Ghost and the Darkness『ゴースト＆ダークネス』(1996年公開. 19世紀末の実話である, アフリカの人食いライオン2頭と2人の男の戦いを描く. 主演マイケル・ダグラス, ヴァル・キルマー.)

_____ minutes _____ seconds

READING COMPREHENSION

Circle the letter of the best answer.

1. How are lions different from other cats?
   a. Males and females look different.
   b. Many zoos keep them.
   c. Lions are from Africa.
   d. Lions are one of the most popular animals at zoos.

2. Male lions . . .
   a. are smaller than females.
   b. are more popular than females.
   c. weigh less than most people.
   d. have manes.

3. Female lions . . .
   a. are larger than males.
   b. can break the back of an animal with one bite.
   c. need to drink water every day.
   d. have manes.

4. How many large animals does one lion usually kill for food in one year?
   a. less than 5
   b. between 5 and 10
   c. between 10 and 20
   d. more than 20

5. Lions can live without water for . . .
   a. a few days.
   b. a week.
   c. a month.
   d. a year.

LISTENING COMPREHENSION   03

Listen to the CD and fill in the blanks.

Lions are different from other cats because it is easy to tell if a lion is male or (1)_____. The male lion has a (2)_____ of hair around its face. Lions have strong mouths. They can break an animal's back with one (3)_____. Lions can also (4)_____ water for a long time, so they have no trouble (5)_____ dry times.

VOCABULARY REINFORCEMENT

Circle the letter of the best answer.

1. My brother is very _____. He can carry me on his back.
   a. popular
   b. male
   c. strong
   d. old

2. Without question, male and female fish are hard to tell _____.
   a. from
   b. with
   c. apart
   d. them

3. Be careful! That dog sometimes _____ people.
   a. bites
   b. weighs
   c. tells
   d. goes without

4. Fast food restaurants are more _____ with young people than with older people.
   a. popular
   b. poor
   c. female
   d. wild

5. I can never tell if a cat is _____ or female.
   a. mane
   b. dry
   c. collar
   d. male

IDIOMS

Find each idiom in the story and translate the sentences into Japanese.

1. (   ) (   ) = なしですます，〜なしで生きる
   How long can a person (   ) (   ) water?

2. (   ) (   ) = 確かに，間違いなく
   (   ) (   ), Fred was the right person for the job.

3. (   ) (things) (   ) = 〜を区別する，〜の違いがわかる．
   Lucy and Emily are twins. No one can (   ) them (   ).

2 RAMEN
ラーメン

　ラーメンは日本人の国民食と言われています．ラーメンには，醤油・味噌・塩・豚骨など様々な種類がありますが，みなさんはどの味のラーメンが好きですか？　人はどうしてラーメンが好きなのでしょうか？日本以外ではどの国の人たちがラーメンを食べるのでしょうか？

TARGET VOCABULARY

Look up each word in a dictionary and match it with the closest meaning.

1. fancy　　　　_____ (　)
2. instant　　　_____ (　)
3. traditional　_____ (　)
4. pour　　　　_____ (　)
5. spread　　　_____ (　)

a. in the same way that was used in the past
b. made to look or taste better; not plain
c. to move in all directions away from a starting place
d. to drop water or liquid out of one container into or onto something
e. needing only a little time and effort to make

READING PASSAGE

1   Ramen noodles are yellow noodles that originally came from China. They became a popular street food in Japan in the early 1900s. Then, after **World War II**, ramen became even more popular in Japan. At that time, Japan did not have much food at all. Ramen was cheap and good, so more and more people began eating it.

   In the 1950s, **Momofuku Ando**, the man who started **Nissin Food Products Co., Ltd.** in Japan, had an idea. He wanted to make dried ramen noodles. People could **pour** hot water over these noodles, wait a few minutes, and then eat them. It would be **instant** ramen! It was not easy, but finally Ando came up with a way to make instant ramen. Japanese people loved it! Soon other companies were copying Ando's idea. Not long after that, instant ramen **spread** to other countries.

   Today, people all around the world enjoy ramen. In fact, people eat about 40 **billion** bowls, cups, or packs of ramen every year!

   But the story of ramen does not end there. Ramen is now moving from streets and instant bowls to good restaurants. All kinds of meats, vegetables, and **spices** are being added to ramen. And people are choosing noodle bars over sushi bars for a nice dinner out these days.

   So whether you want **traditional**, quick, or **fancy** ramen, you can find it. Just look on the street, in a store, or in a restaurant near you.

                                                                                          240 words

World War II「第二次世界大戦」　**Momofuku Ando**「安藤百福」(日清食品株式会社創業者でチキンラーメンを開発した.)　**Nissin Food Products Co., Ltd.**「日清食品株式会社」(1958年創業で人気商品はカップヌードル.)　**billion**「10億」　**spice**「スパイス」

_____ minutes _____ seconds

READING COMPREHENSION

Circle the letter of the best answer.

1. This reading is about . . .
    a. the history of ramen.
    b. a man who ate a lot of ramen.
    c. the way to cook ramen.
    d. kinds of ramen.

2. What became popular in Japan after World War II?
    a. Chinese ramen
    b. Ramen with meat
    c. Instant ramen
    d. Street ramen

3. Who was Momofuku Ando?
    a. A businessman
    b. A restaurant owner
    c. A chef
    d. A soldier in World War II

4. Which of these sentences is true?
    a. Ando thought people would not like instant ramen.
    b. Instant ramen was first made by accident.
    c. Other Japanese companies copied Nissin's new food.
    d. The Nissin company was started in 1950.

5. Which of the following kinds of ramen is NOT mentioned?
    a. Instant ramen
    b. Street ramen
    c. Restaurant-style ramen
    d. Sushi ramen

LISTENING COMPREHENSION 05

Listen to the CD and fill in the blanks.

Ramen noodles are a famous food from Japan. In the 1950s, a Japanese company came up with a way to make (1)_____ ramen noodles. People just needed to (2) _____ water over the noodles and wait for a few minutes. Instant ramen was a big hit in Japan, and it soon (3)_____ to other countries. These days, restaurants are making (4) _____ ramen with all kinds of meats, vegetables, and other things in it. It is not (5) _____ ramen, but some people think it is better!

7

VOCABULARY REINFORCEMENT

Circle the letter of the best answer.

1. I like to read _____ books, but I enjoy books about science and nature the most.
    a. all kinds of
    b. along with
    c. at all
    d. without question

2. My father does not like _____ soup. He makes soup slowly using fresh vegetables.
    a. cheap
    b. instant
    c. popular
    d. traditional

3. The Internet helps new ideas _____ around the world quickly.
    a. walk
    b. spread
    c. pour
    d. popular

4. Some people enjoy growing _____ in their gardens.
    a. dinners
    b. meats
    c. noodles
    d. vegetables

5. The little girl _____ water on her brother's head.
    a. added
    b. copied
    c. poured
    d. spread

IDIOMS

Find each idiom in the story and translate the sentences into Japanese.

1. (　　　) (　　　) = (否定文で) まったく〜ない
    My hand hurt after I fell, but the next day it did not hurt (　　　) (　　　).

2. (　　　) (　　　) (　　　) = 思いつく
    She (　　　) (　　　) (　　　) a good idea for the party. (過去形で)

3. (　　　) (　　　) (　　　) = 様々な種類の
    You can find (　　　) (　　　) (　　　) toys in the store's toy department.

3 THE LEANING TOWER

ピサの斜塔

　今回は，世界遺産としても有名なイタリアのピサの斜塔の話です．世界一傾いている建物としてギネスブックに掲載されたこともあるピサの斜塔ですが，いつ頃建てられ，どうして傾いてしまったのでしょうか？そして近い将来，その傾きが原因で倒れてしまうのでしょうか？

TARGET VOCABULARY

Look up each word in a dictionary and match it with the closest meaning.

1. bell　　　　_____ (　)
2. lean　　　　_____ (　)
3. sink　　　　_____ (　)
4. tower　　　_____ (　)
5. mistake　　_____ (　)

a. go down slowly; go into the ground or underwater
b. a tall, thin building
c. a hollow metal object that makes a nice sound when hit
d. not be straight; bend to one side
e. something wrong or incorrect

READING PASSAGE

1   Why does **the Leaning Tower of Pisa** in Italy **lean**? It leans because of a **mistake**. It has leaned almost since the day the tower was built.

   In 1173, the people of Pisa, Italy, wanted to build a **bell tower**. They wanted the tower to be the most beautiful bell tower in all of Italy. The city also needed a
5 bell tower because the church did not have one.

   However, there was a problem. As soon as the third floor of the building was finished, the tower started to lean. **Builders** tried to make the building straight again as they added more floors, but they could not figure out how to make it stop leaning. When the building was finished in 1350, it had eight floors and was
10 54.5 meters tall.

   After it was built, the tower continued to lean by another millimeter every year. By 1990, it was leaning by about four meters to one side. It was also slowly **sinking** into the ground. Many people became worried that it would soon fall apart.

15 In 1998, repair works began on the tower. Workers took nearly three years to move it back by 45 centimeters. It is still leaning, but it is now safe.

204 words

Notes

the Leaning Tower of Pisa「ピサの斜塔」   bell tower「鐘塔」   builder「建築業者」

_____ minutes _____ seconds

READING COMPREHENSION

Circle the letter of the best answer.

1. Why did the people of Pisa want to build the tower?
    a. They needed a new church.
    b. They needed a bell tower.
    c. They wanted to build the tallest tower in Italy.
    d. They wanted to build a leaning tower.

2. When did the tower begin to lean?
    a. from the first day it was built
    b. after the third floor was built
    c. after the last floor was built
    d. 180 years after it was built

3. When was the tower finished?
    a. in 1173
    b. in 1180
    c. in 1350
    d. in 1474

4. Before being repaired, the tower leaned every year by another . . .
    a. 1 millimeter.
    b. 54.5 millimeters.
    c. 45 centimeters.
    d. 4 meters.

5. Which of the following is NOT true about the tower?
    a. It was sinking into the ground.
    b. It was repaired between 1990 and 1998.
    c. People were worried it might fall apart.
    d. It has eight floors today.

LISTENING COMPREHENSION 07

Listen to the CD and fill in the blanks.

The Leaning Tower of Pisa does not stand (1) _____ . It actually (2) _____ to one side. The tower does this because of a (3) _____ . Even before the whole (4) _____ was finished, it started to lean. As soon as (5) _____ finished the third floor of the tower, it began to lean.

VOCABULARY REINFORCEMENT

Circle the letter of the words that best match the words in *italics*.

1. Sam *discovered* his mistake after he finished the test.
   a. corrected
   b. found
   c. wrote
   d. forgot

2. I need a new car because my old one is about to *fall apart*.
   a. have an accident
   b. be repaired
   c. be sold
   d. break down

3. Alice *gave up* before she finished the test.
   a. began trying
   b. went out
   c. stopped trying
   d. turned into

4. Someone should *invent* a faster way to travel between countries.
   a. make
   b. give
   c. try
   d. fix

5. I went to bed *as soon as* I got home.
   a. then
   b. during
   c. just before
   d. just after

IDIOMS

Find each idiom in the story and translate the sentences into Japanese.

1. (   ) (   ) (   ) = すぐに
   (   ) (   ) (   ) Ann finished her work, she went home.

2. (   ) (   ) = 壊れる，ばらばらになる
   Craig's car (   ) (   ) after only three years.（過去形で）

3. (   ) (   ) = わかる，（問題を）解く
   Did you (   ) (   ) the answer yourself?

A SMART DOG

賢いワンちゃん

みなさんは家でペットを飼っていますか？ ペットとして人気があるのは犬や猫ですね．「チョコ，ごはんだよ」などと言葉でペットとコミュニケーションを取っている人もたくさんいます．今回登場するコリー犬もどうやら言葉を理解するようです．どれくらい賢いワンちゃんなのか確かめてみましょう．

TARGET VOCABULARY

Look up each word in a dictionary and match it with the closest meaning.

1. certain　　　_____　( )
2. language　　_____　( )
3. owner　　　_____　( )
4. train　　　　_____　( )
5. researcher　_____　( )

a. a person who has something known to be his or hers
b. what people use to give information to others
c. exact; specific
d. a person who studies or looks carefully at things
e. to teach an animal (or someone) to do something

13

READING PASSAGE

Rico is a **collie** who lives in Germany. His **owners trained** him from a young age to find his **toys**. When they say the name of a **certain** toy, Rico can find it. In fact, he seems to know the names of 200 toys!

Some **researchers** in Germany wanted to test Rico. They put his toys in a room and then told him to go into the room and find a certain toy. Since nobody was in the room with Rico, he had no help from anyone finding the right toy. The researchers did this test forty **times**. Rico found the right toy thirty-seven times!

Then the researchers tried something else. They put seven of Rico's toys in the room plus one new toy that Rico had never seen before. Then they told Rico to go into the room and get the new toy. This new toy had a name Rico had never heard before. Rico found the right toy seven out of ten times!

Researchers cannot really say that Rico knows words or **language**. However, these tests seem to show that Rico can think about what he hears and what he knows. In fact, Rico seems to think and remember things as well as a three-year-old child.

From these tests, animal researchers know one thing for sure. Rico has given them a lot to think about.

227 words

Notes

collie「コリー犬」 toy「おもちゃ」 times「～回」

_____ minutes _____ seconds

READING COMPREHENSION

Circle the letter of the best answer.

1. A good title for the passage is . . .
   a. German Collies Are the Smartest Dogs
   b. Rico Surprises Researchers
   c. How Dogs Use Language
   d. The Best Toys for Collies

2. What is Rico good at?
   a. Catching things
   b. Finding things
   c. Counting things
   d. Putting things in order

3. What did researchers ask Rico to do at first?
   a. Bring a certain toy out of a room
   b. Name toys plus put them away
   c. Choose a toy that he liked playing with
   d. Put his toys into his room

4. How many times did Rico go into the room to find a new toy he did not know?
   a. Seven
   b. Ten
   c. Thirty-seven
   d. Forty

5. Why were researchers surprised by what they saw?
   a. Rico always knew which toys were his and which were not.
   b. Rico seems to remember things as well as a young child.
   c. Rico showed that he understands language.
   d. Rico worked very hard without help from his owner.

LISTENING COMPREHENSION 09

Listen to the CD and fill in the blanks.

Rico is a collie in Germany. Some (1)_____ wanted to see how smart this dog is. They put all of Rico's toys into a room. Then they told the dog to go into the room and find a (2)_____ toy. Rico could not get help from his owner. Thirty-seven times (3)_____ forty, Rico found the right toy! (4)_____, in another test, he could often find a toy he never heard the name of before. Researchers are not sure that this shows that Rico knows their (5)_____, but it does give the researchers a lot to think about.

VOCABULARY REINFORCEMENT

Circle the letter of the best answer.

1. How did you _____ your bird to eat out of your hand?
   a. lean
   b. pour
   c. spread
   d. train

2. I was looking for a _____ book about lions, but the library did not have it.
   a. certain
   b. plus
   c. right
   d. straight

3. More than six _____ worked together on the project.
   a. features
   b. researchers
   c. towers
   d. zoos

4. Learn all of the words in the list because they will be on the test _____.
   a. as soon as
   b. at all
   c. for sure
   d. out of ten

5. You should do the math problem again. I see a _____ in your work.
   a. language
   b. mistake
   c. owner
   d. toy

IDIOMS

Find each idiom in the story and translate the sentences into Japanese.

1. (number) (   ) (   ) (number) (   ) = 〜回のうち〜回
   Nine (   ) (   ) ten (   ), the bus arrives within five minutes of its scheduled time.

2. (   ) (   ) = 〜について考える
   I did not have to (   ) (   ) the question. It was easy to answer.

3. (   ) (   ) = 確実に，確かに
   You will get a good grade in the class (   ) (   ) if you do well on the final exam.

5 TWENTY-FIRST CENTURY BOOKS

電子書籍

　昔は電車の中で本を読む人をよく見かけました．最近では，本の代わりにタブレットで読書をする人が増えています．そう，電子書籍のことです．電子書籍は普通の書籍よりも便利な点があります．まず何十冊あっても重さは変わりません．文字の大きさを指の操作で簡単に変えることができます．他にはどんなことができるのでしょうか？

TARGET VOCABULARY

Look up each word in a dictionary and match it with the closest meaning.

1. device   _____ ( )   a. a small machine or tool
2. electronic   _____ ( )   b. to keep for future use
3. feature   _____ ( )   c. most likely; there is a good chance that
4. store   _____ ( )   d. a special or important part
5. probably   _____ ( )   e. related to electricity

READING PASSAGE

    Probably you have seen someone reading a book on an **electronic** reading **device. Over the past few years**, these small computers have become more popular. For that reason, more companies that make traditional paper books are now making **electronic books** (ebooks). Most ebooks are the same as paper books, but people download a file into a reading device rather than buying the paper book. This way they can carry many books.

    Book companies are adding special **features** to some ebooks. These extra features might include sound files, picture files, or video files. When the readers click on these files, they learn more about the book, the story, or the writer.

    The latest electronic readers are smaller and cheaper, but they are also much more powerful. They can **store** much more information, so writers and book companies can do more with their ebooks. They do not want to just add files to a completed book. They are making the sound, picture, and video files part of the story. Readers need these files to understand the whole story. Readers can even change the story.

    Readers already have a lot of books to choose from. If they can change the way stories end, they will have even more choice!

206 words

over the past few years 「この数年間」　electronic book 「電子書籍」

_____ minutes _____ seconds

READING COMPREHENSION

Circle the letter of the best answer.

1. This reading is about …
    a. books about the future.
    b. books written after 1999.
    c. electronic books.
    d. popular writers today.

2. Which sentence is true about the devices described in the passage?
    a. You can use them to read ebooks.
    b. They change paper books into ebooks.
    c. You can use them to make videos.
    d. They weigh less than a paper book.

3. According to the passage, what special feature might some ebooks include?
    a. copies of the paper book
    b. extra files
    c. devices for other ebooks
    d. other writers' ebooks

4. Which of the following ebooks is NOT mentioned in the passage?
    a. an ebook that has sold over one million copies
    b. an ebook that is only text
    c. an ebook with a sound file that tells part of the story
    d. an ebook with a video about the writer

5. How are some ebooks today different than older ebooks?
    a. Companies sell them in many files.
    b. Readers can change the stories.
    c. Devices make them easier to read.
    d. Writers do not finish them.

LISTENING COMPREHENSION

Listen to the CD and fill in the blanks.

These days, rather than reading paper books, people are now reading (1) _____ books (ebooks). These ebooks can be read using special (2)_____. A person just downloads the (3)_____ into his or her device to read it. Some ebooks include extra (4)_____. Readers can choose from picture or sound files included with the ebook. Or they can (5)_____ video files to learn about the writer or other information.

VOCABULARY REINFORCEMENT

Circle the letter of the word or phrase that best matches the word(s) in *italics*.

1. I *keep* my books on this reader. Now my bag is not so heavy.
   a. store
   b. train
   c. pour
   d. spread

2. My brother will *most likely* study in the library after school.
   a. electronically
   b. only
   c. probably
   d. usually

3. One *good thing* about the new movie theater is that it has a great sound system.
   a. company
   b. device
   c. feature
   d. video

4. Send me an email with the *saved data* after you get home tonight.
   a. collar
   b. computer
   c. ebook
   d. file

5. I think I will ride my bike to school *instead of* taking the bus.
   a. no problem
   b. rather than
   c. the same as
   d. without question

IDIOMS

Find each idiom in the story and translate the sentences into Japanese.

1. (   ) (   ) = 〜の代わりに，〜ではなく
   Let us stay home tonight and watch a DVD (   ) (   ) going to a movie theater.

2. (   ) (   ) = クリックする
   After you type an email message, please (   ) (   ) the "send" button.

3. (   ) (   ) = 〜から選ぶ
   I want to buy a new computer, but there are so many to (   ) (   )!

6 VALENTINE'S DAY

バレンタイン・デー

　2月になると恋をしている人たちはそわそわします．どうしてかといえば，それはもちろん14日にバレンタイン・デーがあるからですね．どうして2月14日がバレンタイン・デーになったのでしょうか？　また，日本では，一般的に女性から男性にチョコレートが贈られますが，世界ではどうなのでしょうか？

TARGET VOCABULARY

Look up each word in a dictionary and match it with the closest meaning.

1. message　　_____ (　) 　a. an idea you think is true
2. gloves　　　_____ (　) 　b. do something special for a happy day or event
3. celebrate　 _____ (　) 　c. something you wear to keep your hands warm
4. festival　　 _____ (　) 　d. a short written or spoken note
5. belief　　　 _____ (　) 　e. a happy day or event that people celebrate

READING PASSAGE

1 February 14 is a day for people who have fallen in love. On this day, these men and women give gifts and cards to each other to **celebrate** Valentine's Day.

At first, February 14 was the old Roman **festival**, **Lupercalia**. Then, on February 14, 270 **A.D.**, a man named Valentine was killed by the **Romans** because of his Christian **beliefs**.

Before Valentine was killed, he fell in love with the daughter of his **jailer** and would pass notes to her. His final note read, "From your Valentine." Later, February 14 became known as Saint Valentine's Day.

Since then, people in love around the world have given gifts and cards to each other on Saint Valentine's Day. **Gloves**, chocolates, and even underwear have all been popular as gifts.

Valentine cards did not become popular until the 1750s. The first Valentine cards were made **by hand**. People wrote their own words on the cards, usually a kind or funny **message**. Cards made by machines became more popular around 1850. All of a sudden, Valentine's Day became a big holiday for people who made and sold cards.

Now, every year around February 14, cards and chocolates fill stores around the world, for all the people who have fallen in love.

207 words

Notes

Lupercalia「ルペルカーリア祭」(牧神ルペルクスのために行われた祭典.) **A.D.**「西暦」 **Roman**「古代ローマ人」 **jailer**「看守」 **by hand**「手製で」

_____ minutes _____ seconds

READING COMPREHENSION

Circle the letter of the best answer.

1. A good title for this reading passage is . . .
    a. The History of Valentine's Day   c. The Most Romantic Valentine's Day Ever
    b. Why People Fall in Love   d. Modern Valentine's Day Customs

2. Who was Saint Valentine?
    a. a man who killed someone   c. a Christian
    b. a Roman god   d. a man who made cards

3. What was Lupercalia?
    a. a Christian festival   c. a type of card
    b. a Roman festival   d. Saint Valentine's real name

4. When did Valentine cards first become popular?
    a. about 270   c. about 1850
    b. about 1750   d. February 14th

5. Why is Saint Valentine thought to be romantic?
    a. He was killed by the Romans.
    b. He fell in love with his jailer.
    c. He passed love notes to the daughter of his jailer.
    d. He gave cards and chocolates to all his friends.

LISTENING COMPREHENSION 13

Listen to the CD and fill in the blanks.

When two people (1)_____, they may give gifts to each other on Valentine's Day. Long ago, February 14 was called Lupercalia, a Roman festival, but now it is known as Saint Valentine's Day and is (2)_____ around the world. On this day in the past, people often gave a gift such as (3)_____ to the person they loved, and now people usually write (4)_____ in cards as well.

23

VOCABULARY REINFORCEMENT

Circle the letter of the best answer.

1. Mary put on her _____ because her hands were cold.
   a. underwear
   b. collar
   c. chocolates
   d. gloves

2. Irish people _____ Saint Patrick's Day on March 17.
   a. believe
   b. celebrate
   c. give
   d. are known as

3. She wasn't home when I phoned, so I left her a _____.
   a. card
   b. prize
   c. brain
   d. message

4. In Japan, there are a lot of _____ in summer.
   a. cards
   b. messages
   c. festivals
   d. celebrates

5. _____ the lights went out, and someone screamed.
   a. Turn out
   b. Now and then
   c. All of a sudden
   d. As soon as

IDIOMS

Find each idiom in the story and translate the sentences into Japanese.

1. (　　) (　　) (　　) (　　) = 突然
   (　　) (　　) (　　) (　　), the lights went out. It was very dark.

2. (　　) (　　) = 最初に, まず
   Sara didn't like Matt (　　) (　　), but then she got to know him.

3. (　　) (　　) (　　) = 恋をする
   It is wonderful to (　　) (　　) (　　).

24

7 THE TAJ MAHAL

ある愛の形

　最近，日本では富士山が世界遺産に登録されましたが，世界遺産を見たことはありますか？　インドの世界遺産ではタージ・マハルが有名ですが，写真の通り，非常に大きな建造物です．タージ・マハルはいつ建造されたのでしょうか？　また，誰がなんのために建てたのでしょうか？

TARGET VOCABULARY

Look up each word in a dictionary and match it with the closest meaning.

1. bury　　　_____ (　)　a. the study of things that happened in the past
2. cruel　　 _____ (　)　b. the covering on top of a building
3. marble　　_____ (　)　c. causing pain to other people
4. roof　　　_____ (　)　d. a stone used in buildings
5. history　　_____ (　)　e. put a dead person in the ground

READING PASSAGE

Shah Jahan built **the Taj Mahal** in Agra, India, in the 1600s. He wanted to make a beautiful place where he could **bury** his wife.

Mumtaz Mahal was only one of Shah Jahan's wives, but he liked her the most. After Mumtaz Mahal died, the Shah built for her the Taj Mahal, a beautiful building made of white **marble** and covered by a white round **roof**.

It took twenty-two years to complete all of the work on the Taj Mahal. Today, it is one of the most famous things to see in India. **The Jumna River** runs beside the north wall of the Taj Mahal, and a smaller river runs through a beautiful garden that grows inside the building.

People who study **history** have found out that Shah Jahan was also a **cruel** man. After the Taj Mahal was completed, Shah Jahan killed the man who made the Taj Mahal because he did not want him to ever build anything more beautiful than the Taj Mahal. The Shah also cut off the hands of all of the artists who took part in building the Taj Mahal.

As for Shah Jahan, when he died he was also buried in the Taj Mahal, next to his wife.

205 words

Notes

Shah Jahan「シャー・ジャハーン」(第五代ムガル皇帝. 1628年皇帝に即位.) the Taj Mahal「タージ・マハル」(シャー・ジャハーンが建造した白大理石の霊廟.) the Jumna River「ヤムナー川」(ガンジス川最大の支流.)

_____ minutes _____ seconds

READING COMPREHENSION

Circle the letter of the best answer.

1. Why did Shah Jahan build the Taj Mahal?
    a. He needed a new place to live.
    b. He liked beautiful gardens.
    c. He wanted to bury his wife there.
    d. His wife wanted to live in a beautiful building.

2. Who was Mumtaz Mahal?
    a. one of the Shah's wives
    b. a person who studied history
    c. the man who made the Taj Mahal
    d. an artist who worked on the Taj Mahal

3. What can you NOT see when you visit the Taj Mahal?
    a. the Jumna River
    b. a round bell tower
    c. a beautiful garden
    d. the place where Mumtaz Mahal is buried

4. Why did Shah Jahan kill the man who made the Taj Mahal?
    a. The Shah didn't like the Taj Mahal.
    b. The man made a mistake.
    c. The Shah did not want him to make another building.
    d. The man did not finish the building.

5. What did Shah Jahan do that makes people think he was a cruel man?
    a. He buried his wife.
    b. He built the Taj Mahal.
    c. He cut off the hands of many artists.
    d. He killed one of his wives.

LISTENING COMPREHENSION

Listen to the CD and fill in the blanks.

Shah Jahan (1)_____ the Taj Mahal for his wife, Mumtaz. He (2)_____ her inside the Taj Mahal. This building is famous for its beautiful round white (3)_____. People who study history are not surprised to (4)_____ that Shah Jahan killed the man who made the Taj Mahal. Shah Jahan was sometimes very (5)_____.

VOCABULARY REINFORCEMENT

Circle the letter of the best answer.

1. The boy jumped off the _____, and broke his leg.
   a. bell
   b. cage
   c. roof
   d. history

2. If you buy the expensive one, it won't _____ when you use it.
   a. find out
   b. fall apart
   c. figure out
   d. give up

3. Some people think it is _____ to keep a bird in a cage.
   a. intelligent
   b. popular
   c. successful
   d. cruel

4. The dog _____ the toy in the garden.
   a. completed
   b. buried
   c. surprised
   d. found out

5. I _____ an interesting new bookstore.
   a. discovered
   b. buried
   c. took part in
   d. chewed

IDIOMS

Find each idiom in the story and translate the sentences into Japanese.

1. (　　　) (　　　) = 〜といえば，〜については
   (　　　) (　　　) Jim, he speaks three languages.

2. (　　　) (　　　) = 〜について知る，〜がわかる
   When you (　　　) (　　　) her name, please tell me.

3. (　　　) (　　　) (　　　) = 〜に参加する，〜に加わる
   Wendy (　　　) (　　　) (　　　) the English club in high school.（過去形で）

8 A COMPUTER PROBLEM

コンピューターのホットな問題

みなさんはデスクトップパソコンとノートパソコンのどちらをよく使いますか？ 現在，国内出荷台数ではノートパソコンが圧倒的に多いようです．電車でもノートパソコンを使用している人をよく見かけます．手軽に運べて，どこでもメール・インターネット・仕事ができる便利なノートパソコンですが，欠点はなんでしょうか？

TARGET VOCABULARY

Look up each word in a dictionary and match it with the closest meaning.

1. avoid _____ ( )
2. bare _____ ( )
3. lap _____ ( )
4. notice _____ ( )
5. protect _____ ( )

a. the top of your legs when you are sitting down
b. to see and take time to think about
c. to keep from harm or injury
d. without a covering
e. to try not to experience; to take action to stay away from

READING PASSAGE 16

1   Computers make people's lives easier. People can use their computers for working, shopping, or playing games. **Laptop computers** make people's lives even easier! Instead of just using a computer at home, people can take laptops anywhere. They can work, shop, or play games at any place at any time. But
5   there is a problem with laptops. People can be burned by them!

People who sit with laptops on their legs for hours and hours have **noticed** they get dark marks on their legs. The hot laptop is **toasting** the skin. Doctors have noticed more people show up with "toasted skin **syndrome**." They use their laptops every day for hours and hours for a month or more and this results
10 in a **burn**. The marks are not dangerous, but they look strange because they are just in one spot on people's legs.

Companies that make computers tell people not to let warm computers touch **bare** skin for a long time. Wearing pants and putting a laptop's case under the laptop is usually enough to **protect** one's skin from the computer's heat. But the
15 best way to **avoid** toasted skin is not to put a laptop on your **lap** when you use it for a long time.

205 words

laptop computer「ノートパソコン」 toast「～をこんがり焼く」 syndrome「症候群」 burn「やけど」

_____ minutes _____ seconds

READING COMPREHENSION

Circle the letter of the best answer.

1. This reading is about . . .
    a. a problem that companies may have.
    b. a problem that pants may have.
    c. a problem that games may have.
    d. a problem that people may have.

2. What does toasted skin syndrome result in?
    a. a burn
    b. a hot laptop
    c. a dangerous problem
    d. a way to protect your skin

3. How long does a person need to sit with a laptop on his or her lap to experience this problem?
    a. less than 30 minutes
    b. a few hours
    c. about one week
    d. more than a month

4. Which of the following is NOT true about toasted skin syndrome?
    a. It covers a person's whole leg.
    b. It is not a dangerous problem.
    c. It is a burn.
    d. It looks like a brown spot.

5. What can be guessed about the people who got toasted skin syndrome?
    a. They did not protect their laps well while using their laptops.
    b. They felt pain when their pants touched the burns on their legs.
    c. They tried to make the laptop companies pay the doctors' bills.
    d. They were working outdoors with their laptops.

LISTENING COMPREHENSION

Listen to the CD and fill in the blanks.

People can use laptop computers (1) _____ desktop computers to work in various places. When they use laptops, they should not sit with their computers on their laps. The bottom of a laptop can get hot and burn a person's (2)_____ skin. Doctors call this problem "(3)_____ skin syndrome." It is easy to (4)_____ this problem. A person just needs to (5)_____ his or her lap with thick clothes or a laptop case. Then these kinds of burns will not show up on the person's legs.

VOCABULARY REINFORCEMENT

Circle the letter of the word or phrase that best matches the word(s) in *italics*.

1. The baby was happy as long as she was sitting on her mother's *legs*.
   a. festival
   b. history
   c. lap
   d. syndrome

2. My brother *escapes from* washing the dishes by hiding in his room.
   a. avoids
   b. celebrates
   c. protects
   d. notices

3. She put the old pictures in a box to *keep them safe*.
   a. avoid them
   b. bury them
   c. celebrate them
   d. protect them

4. The *cooked* bread was a little hard, but it was delicious.
   a. bare
   b. cruel
   c. straight
   d. toasted

5. My uncle *appeared* at our front door last night without telling us he was coming to visit.
   a. fell in love
   b. found out
   c. showed up
   d. took part in

IDIOMS

Find each idiom in the story and translate the sentences into Japanese.

1. (   ) (   ) = 〜の代わりに
   She called her friend (   ) (   ) sending her an email.

2. (   ) (   ) = 現れる，やって来る
   My teacher usually (   ) (   ) five minutes before class starts.

3. (   ) (   ) (   ) = 一つの場所で
   The store near my apartment is excellent. I can find everything I need (   ) (   ) (   ).

9 THE MOBIUS BAND

不思議な輪

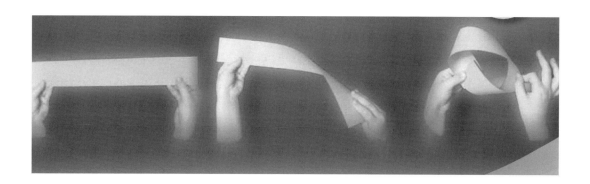

　写真を見てください．何を作っていると思いますか？　一番右の形ですが，なにか変っていませんか？　これはメビウスの輪といいます．この奇妙な形状の輪は，ある不思議な特徴を持っています．それは何なのでしょうか？　話を読んでから，メビウスの輪を作ってみるのもいいかもしれませんね．

TARGET VOCABULARY

Look up each word in a dictionary and match it with the closest meaning.

1. twist　　　_____ (　)　a. to show that something is true or real
2. connect　 _____ (　)　b. unusual or difficult to understand
3. prove　　 _____ (　)　c. the outside layer of something, or the top
4. strange　 _____ (　)　　　of something
5. surface　 _____ (　)　d. to put or join together
　　　　　　　　　　　　　　　e. to turn; bend around each other

READING PASSAGE

1 Take any long piece of paper. Now glue the ends of the paper together. You have made a ring.

Take a second long piece of paper. **Twist** the paper once and glue the ends together. Now you have made a **Mobius band**. For people who study math, this
5 band is special.

This **strange** band was first made in the 1800s by a German man named **August Mobius**. Mr. Mobius studied math. He wanted to find a way to **prove** how this band works with math. Believe it or not, this band has only one **surface**. You can find this out for yourself.

10 If you draw a line along the surface of the paper before you twist and glue it, the line is only on one side of the paper. The paper has two surfaces. However, if you draw a line after you make the Mobius band, you can follow the line around all sides of the paper. In other words, the Mobius band must have only one surface.

15 It is also kind of fun to see what happens when you cut the band. If you cut the Mobius band in half along the line you drew, you do not get two Mobius bands. Instead, after you cut the band, it turns into one large, twisted ring. Then, if you cut this ring in half along the middle of the band again, you get two **connected** Mobius bands.

237 words

Notes

Mobius band「メビウスの輪」(表裏の区別がない不思議な輪.) **August Mobius**「アウグスト・メビウス」(ドイツの数学者でメビウスの輪を発見した.)

_____ minutes _____ seconds

READING COMPREHENSION

Circle the letter of the best answer.

1. What is a Mobius band?
   a. a musical group
   b. a type of German paper
   c. an interesting twisted ring
   d. a person who studies math

2. Which sentence about August Mobius is NOT true? August Mobius . . .
   a. studied math.
   b. discovered a special type of glue.
   c. was a German.
   d. made the first Mobius band.

3. How can you prove that the Mobius band has only one side?
   a. cut it
   b. draw a line along it
   c. glue it
   d. twist it

4. What do you get if you cut a Mobius band along the line you drew?
   a. a large, twisted ring
   b. two long pieces of paper
   c. two Mobius bands
   d. a short piece of paper

5. What do you get if you cut the Mobius band in half again?
   a. one large twisted ring
   b. a long piece of paper
   c. two Mobius bands
   d. a short piece of paper

LISTENING COMPREHENSION   19

Listen to the CD and fill in the blanks.

If you (1)_____ a strip of paper and glue the ends together, you can make a Mobius band. This (2) _____ is very interesting. A Mobius band has only one (3) _____ . If you draw a line along the middle of the band, you can (4)_____ this for yourself. You will see something (5)_____ when you cut it along the line you drew.

35

VOCABULARY REINFORCEMENT

Circle the letter of the best answer.

1. I am broke this week. _____, I cannot afford to go to the cinema.
   a. In other words
   b. Now and then
   c. Off and on
   d. At first

2. The job, which seemed small, _____ a lot of work.
   a. came true
   b. took part in
   c. turned into
   d. figured out

3. The police _____ that the man was the killer.
   a. connected
   b. proved
   c. twisted
   d. turned into

4. Can you _____ this computer to that printer?
   a. lean
   b. bury
   c. twist
   d. connect

5. I have studied Spanish _____ for many years.
   a. in other words
   b. at first
   c. off and on
   d. by accident

IDIOMS

Find each idiom in the story and translate the sentences into Japanese.

1. (   ) (   ) (   ) = つまり，言い換えると
   Mike is studying. (   ) (   ) (   ), he cannot go to the movie with us.

2. (   ) (   ) = ちょっと
   Nina is (   ) (   ) quiet and shy.

3. (   ) (   ) = 〜になる
   The ugly baby duck (   ) (   ) a beautiful swan.（過去形で）

10 A LONG WEEKEND

休日の落とし穴

　皆さんは，休日に仕事をすることについてどう思いますか？　会社のために少しでも力になりたい人や休日出勤手当が欲しい人は賛成ですね．逆にプライベートの時間を大切にしたい人は反対ですね．今回は，休日に仕事をしたためにある災難に遭遇してしまった人の話です．どんな災難だったのでしょうか？

TARGET VOCABULARY

Look up each word in a dictionary and match it with the closest meaning.

1. terrible　　＿＿＿＿＿（　）
2. dangerous　＿＿＿＿＿（　）
3. tired　　　＿＿＿＿＿（　）
4. shout　　　＿＿＿＿＿（　）
5. elevator　　＿＿＿＿＿（　）

a. large box used to carry people between floors of a building
b. very bad
c. able to hurt someone
d. speak loudly
e. sleepy; feeling weak

37

READING PASSGE

1   Many people have to work on the weekend. Some people do not mind. Other people think it is **terrible**.

One man thinks that working on the weekend can be **dangerous**. He is Graham Coates. Mr. Coates worked in an office in Brighton, England.

5   On Saturday, May 24, 1986, he went to the office to do some work. When he got in the **elevator** to go home, it stopped between floors. Mr. Coates could not get out of the elevator. He **was trapped**! He started to **shout**, but no one heard him. Then Mr. Coates remembered that it was a **holiday** in England. No one was going to come to work until Tuesday!

10   There was nothing for Mr. Coates to do. He had to wait until one of his coworkers came to work and found him. With nothing to eat or drink, Mr. Coates ended up sleeping for most of the time.

Early on Tuesday morning, the **vice president** of the company came into work and found the elevator was not working. When the elevator was opened, Mr.
15   Coates came out cold, weak, and **tired**. He had been in the elevator for sixty-two hours!

Now Mr. Coates says, "I only use elevators if they have telephones in them."

207 words

Notes

was trapped「閉じ込められた」 **holiday**「休日」（ここでは「銀行休日」(Bank Holiday) を指す．銀行休日とは，1871年にイギリスの法律で定められた日曜日以外の法定休日のことで，当時銀行が閉まると商売ができなかったことに由来する．） **vice president**「副社長」

_____ minutes _____ seconds

READING COMPREHENSION

Circle the letter of the best answer.

1. Why could Mr. Coates not get out of the elevator?
    a. It broke down.
    b. It was the weekend.
    c. It was in an office.
    d. It was a holiday.

2. What is NOT a reason why Mr. Coates spent so long in the elevator?
    a. It was a three-day weekend.
    b. He had no food or drink.
    c. The elevator was stuck between two floors.
    d. There was no telephone in the elevator.

3. How long was he in the elevator?
    a. twenty-four hours
    b. sixty-two hours
    c. forty-eight hours
    d. seventy-two hours

4. How was Mr. Coates able to get out of the elevator?
    a. He telephoned his coworkers.
    b. The elevator started again.
    c. The vice president discovered the elevator wasn't working.
    d. His coworkers found him when they came back to work on Monday.

5. What is the best title for this story?
    a. An Interesting Elevator
    b. Elevator Safety
    c. A Busy Weekend
    d. Trapped in an Elevator

LISTENING COMPREHENSION 21

Listen to the CD and fill in the blanks.

A man in England had a (1)_____ experience with an elevator at his office. After he (2)_____ the elevator, it broke down and he was trapped. The man tried to (3)_____ for help, but it was a holiday so no one was in the building. He (4)_____ staying in the elevator for more than sixty hours, without any food or water.

VOCABULARY REINFORCEMENT

Circle the letter of the words that best match the words in *italics*.

1. Did you try the soup? It's *terrible*.
    a. very good
    b. very bad
    c. very cold
    d. very hot

2. The bird's *nest* was very difficult to see up in the tree.
    a. cage
    b. bell
    c. brain
    d. home

3. That dog *is dangerous*.
    a. is tired
    b. is very weak
    c. may bite you
    d. wants some food

4. Everyone was out, so I wrote a *note* for them.
    a. message
    b. festival
    c. belief
    d. bet

5. At the end of the long day, we felt kind of *tired*.
    a. cruel
    b. sleepy
    c. terrible
    d. popular

IDIOMS

Find each idiom in the story and translate the sentences into Japanese.

1. (   ) (   ) (doing something) = 結局〜する（になる）
    Rita always (   ) (   ) washing the dishes. Everyone else is busy.

2. (   ) (   ) = （電車や飛行機など）に乗り込む，乗る
    Sam tried to (   ) (   ) the bus, but the bus was full.

3. (   ) (   ) (   ) = （車やエレベーターなど）から降りる
    Hold the door, please! I need to (   ) (   ) (   ) the elevator on this floor.

11 BREAKFAST

アメリカの朝食

みなさんの好きな朝食はなんですか？ 和食ならごはんと味噌汁，おかずはアジの干物・目玉焼き・納豆などが定番ですね．朝からしっかり食べれば，いいスタートを切ることができます．日本以外の国では，どのような朝食があるか知っていますか？ 今回はアメリカの朝食について学びます．

TARGET VOCABULARY

Look up each word in a dictionary and match it with the closest meaning.

1. war　　　　　_____ (　)　　a. very old
2. ancient　　　_____ (　)　　b. in the same way people in the past did something
3. recipe　　　 _____ (　)
4. serve　　　　_____ (　)　　c. give food (e.g., in a restaurant)
5. traditionally _____ (　)　　d. a fight between different groups or countries
　　　　　　　　　　　　　　　　　　e. instructions for preparing food; steps to help you cook

41

READING PASSAGE

1   Popular breakfast foods in the United States, as in many other countries around the world, include coffee, milk, juice, eggs, and bread. Many people think that some of the other breakfast items **served** in the United States such as pancakes, **bagels**, and donuts are **traditionally** American. However, they actually come
5   from other cultures.

   Pancakes, a thin, flat cake made out of **flour** and often served with **maple syrup**, are a very popular breakfast food in America. The idea of the pancake is very old and they were made in many countries. Records show they were even made long ago in **ancient** China.

10   Bagels, a round, thick bread with a hole in the middle, are also popular for breakfast in America. **Polish people** in the late 1600s came up with the idea for the first bagels, and this new kind of bread soon took off across Eastern Europe.

   In the late 1800s, thousands of **Jews** from Eastern Europe traveled to the United States and brought the **recipe** for bagels with them. Today, New York
15   bagels are said to be the best in the world. Many people have them with cream cheese for breakfast on the go.

   Donuts (also spelled "doughnut" in some countries) came from France. They were served to American soldiers in France during World **War** I. After the war, American soldiers asked cooks in the United States to make donuts for them.
20   Now, served with coffee, they are a very popular breakfast food across the United States.

248 words

Notes

bagels「ベーグル」 flour「小麦粉」 maple syrup「メープルシロップ」 Polish people「ポーランド人」 Jews「ユダヤ人」

 _____ minutes _____ seconds

READING COMPREHENSION

Circle the letter of the best answer.

1. This reading is mainly about . . .
   a. famous places to eat breakfast.
   b. why people in the United States eat breakfast.
   c. the most popular types of pancakes in the United States.
   d. the history of popular breakfast foods in the United States.

2. Which sentence is true for both bagels and donuts?
   a. They both came from Europe.
   b. They are both sweet.
   c. They are both easy to make.
   d. People in New York make them best.

3. Who brought bagels to America?
   a. Polish people
   b. Chinese people
   c. Jewish people
   d. American soldiers

4. Who served donuts to American soldiers during World War I?
   a. French people
   b. other American soldiers
   c. Jewish people
   d. cooks from the United States

5. The oldest breakfast food in the passage is . . .
   a. the pancake.
   b. the bagel.
   c. the donut.
   d. coffee.

LISTENING COMPREHENSION

Listen to the CD and fill in the blanks.

Pancakes, bagels, and donuts are three American breakfast foods that (1)_____ come from other cultures. Pancakes are a very old (2)_____. They were eaten long ago in (3)_____ China. Polish people came up with the idea for bagels in the 1600s. People from Europe brought the (4)_____ for this food to the USA in the late 1800s. Bagels are a very popular food for people eating (5)_____.

43

VOCABULARY REINFORCEMENT

Circle the letter of the word or phrase that best completes the sentence.

1. People think Arthur is very serious, but _____ he is quite funny.
    a. in other words
    b. actually
    c. as for
    d. no matter

2. This restaurant does not _____ wine or beer.
    a. serve
    b. cook
    c. recipe
    d. hide

3. The British Royal family have _____ had weddings at Westminster Abbey in London.
    a. kind of
    b. during
    c. as soon as
    d. traditionally

4. This apple pie is from an old family _____.
    a. serve
    b. recipe
    c. ancient
    d. portrait

5. Tony's grandfather was killed in the _____.
    a. by accident
    b. long ago
    c. portrait
    d. war

IDIOMS

Find each idiom in the story and translate the sentences into Japanese.

1. (   ) (   ) (   ) = 忙しい
    I'm really tired. I've been (   ) (   ) (   ) all day.

2. (   ) (   ) = 昔は
    (   ) (   ), Ireland was completely covered by forest.

3. (   ) (   ) (   ) = (考えなど)を思いつく，(人や事)に追いつく
    Thomas Edison (   ) (   ) (   ) a lot of great inventions.（過去形で）

12 THE WORLD CUP

ワールドカップ

　4年に1度のスポーツの祭典といえば，オリンピックですが，もう一つの有名な大会は何だかわかりますか？　そう，FIFAワールドカップですね．サッカーは世界中で非常に人気の高いスポーツで，日本でも国際大会のTV放送は高い視聴率です．みなさんの好きな選手は誰ですか？

TARGET VOCABULARY

Look up each word in a dictionary and match it with the closest meaning.

1. beat　　　_____　(　)
2. final　　　_____　(　)
3. record　　_____　(　)
4. score　　　_____　(　)
5. tournament _____　(　)

a. set of games to find the best player or team
b. last
c. do better than; win against (someone or something)
d. best in history
e. make a point or goal

READING PASSAGE

1 **Every four years**, the world turns its attention to soccer and **the FIFA World Cup**. The most successful teams have traditionally come from South America and Europe. However, over the years, there have been a number of surprising results.

5 In a famous match in 1950, the USA came up against England, one of the favorites to win the **tournament**. Many of the American players were from college teams.

Surprisingly, the USA won 1-0. Other World Cup surprises were North Korea's win over Italy in 1966, and Cameroon's win over Argentina in 1990.

10 The 2002 FIFA World Cup stands out as probably one of the most surprising World Cup tournaments of all time. In the opening match, Senegal surprised everyone by **beating** France, the World Cup winner in 1998. South Korea, the **co-host country** that year with Japan, made it all the way to **the final four**, before finally losing to Germany. In the **final** game, Brazil ended up winning 2-0
15 against Germany. Brazil set a World Cup **record** by becoming the first team to win seven games in a row. And Brazil's most talented player, **Ronaldo, scored** eight goals in one tournament — more than any other player since 1970.

The tournament of 2010, which was held in South Africa, ended in a match between two teams that had never won the World Cup before. In the final match,
20 Spain beat the Netherlands 1-0 in extra time. This was also the first FIFA World Cup tournament in an African country.

250 words

Notes

every four years「4年ごとに」 **the FIFA World Cup**「FIFA（国際サッカー連盟）ワールドカップ」（4年に1度開催されるサッカーの国際大会．2002年は日本と韓国の共同開催だった．） **co-host country**「共催国」 **the final four**「準決勝」 **Ronaldo**「ロナウド・ルイス・ナザリオ・ジ・リマ」（16歳でデビューして以来長らく活躍した元天才ストライカー．）

＿＿＿ minutes ＿＿＿ seconds

READING COMPREHENSION

Circle the letter of the best answer.

1. What is the best title for the passage?
   a. How the World Cup is Played
   b. The History of Soccer
   c. The Greatest World Cup Players of All Time
   d. Surprises in the World Cup

2. According to the passage, which team has NOT had a surprising win in a World Cup match?
   a. Cameroon
   b. Italy
   c. North Korea
   d. the United States

3. Which team probably surprised people the most in the 2002 World Cup?
   a. Germany
   b. Spain
   c. Japan
   d. South Korea

4. What record did Ronaldo set in the 2002 tournament?
   a. first player to score eight goals
   b. most games played in a World Cup
   c. most goals scored in a World Cup since 1970
   d. oldest player to score in a World Cup

5. What is NOT true about the 2010 World Cup?
   a. A past winner of the World Cup won the tournament.
   b. Spain played in the finals.
   c. The Netherlands lost in extra time.
   d. This was the first time the World Cup was held in South Africa.

LISTENING COMPREHENSION 25

Listen to the CD and fill in the blanks.

In the history of the World Cup, some teams have really (1)_____ fans. A number of times, an unknown team has (2)_____ a well-known team in an important match. This happened several times during the 2002 World Cup. In fact, that year, the South Korean team (3)_____ the final four. Then, in the 2010 World Cup, neither of the two teams that played in the final match had ever won the (4)_____ before. Spain finally won by (5)_____ the only point of the match.

VOCABULARY REINFORCEMENT

Circle the letter of the words that best match the words in *italics*.

1. There will be eight games in the the *sports competition*.
    a. tournament
    b. matches
    c. goal
    d. record

2. The *last* test for the class will be two weeks from today.
    a. connected
    b. final
    c. ancient
    d. valuable

3. Everyone shouted happily when she *got* the winning goal.
    a. beat
    b. expanded
    c. leaned
    d. scored

4. He ran so fast in the race that he broke the *world's best time so far*.
    a. world match
    b. world game
    c. world goal
    d. world record

5. I do not think our team can *win against* the team from Sweden.
    a. beat
    b. celebrate
    c. divorce
    d. score

IDIOMS

Find each idiom in the story and translate the sentences into Japanese.

1. (   ) (one's) (   ) (   ) (something) = 〜に注意を向ける
   Now, please (   ) your (   ) (   ) this painting, and I'll explain a little about it.

2. (   ) (   ) (all the way) (   ) = 〜（到達困難な場所）にたどりつく
   The singer (   ) (   ) (   ) the final round of the competition, but he didn't win.（過去形で）

3. (   ) (   ) (   ) = 〜（困難など）に直面する
   The army (   ) (   ) (   ) 10,000 soldiers in that battle.（過去形で）

13 BLOOD TYPES

血液型で性格判断

親しくなった人に血液型を尋ねて性格判断をしたことはありますか？日本では，血液型によって性格が異なると考える人が多いようです．国によって血液型の構成比率が違いますが，それが原因で国民性が異なるのでしょうか？　世界で一番多い血液型は何型なのでしょうか？

TARGET VOCABULARY

Look up each word in a dictionary and match it with the closest meaning.

1. outgoing _____ ( )   a. interested in knowing about things
2. curious   _____ ( )   b. tells the truth and can be trusted
3. generous _____ ( )   c. different and imaginative
4. honest   _____ ( )   d. friendly and likes talking to and meeting people
5. original _____ ( )   e. happy to give

READING PASSAGE

1   In 1901, **Karl Landsteiner**, an Austrian scientist, discovered that there are four types of blood. These four **blood types** were named A, B, AB, and O. People have one of these four types. Blood type O is the most common around the world. Blood type A is the second most common, and type AB is the least
5   common. If people with type A blood are given type B blood, or people with type B blood are given type A blood, they will probably die.

   In 1927, a Japanese doctor, **Furukawa Takeji**, carried out research and came up with the idea that people with different blood types also had different personalities. He said that people with type A blood are usually calm and serious;
10 people with type B blood are **curious**, cheerful, and **outgoing**; people with type O blood are **generous** and **honest**; while those with type AB blood are often caring, **original**, and careful.

   More recently, a doctor in the United States wrote a book that links blood types and what people eat. For example, his book suggests people with type O
15 blood should eat more meat and less bread. A diet for people with type A blood includes more vegetables. His book, *Eat Right for Your Type*, has been a hit with people who want to lose weight. However, Dr. Peter D'Adamo believes that eating food that matches a person's blood type can do more than help them lose weight. He thinks it will make the person healthier in other ways, too.

253 words

Notes

Karl Landsteiner「カール・ラントシュタイナー」（オーストリアの医学者．血液型を発見した．）　**blood type**「血液型」　**Furukawa Takeji**「古川竹二」（心理学者・教育学者．元東京女子高等師範学校（現在のお茶の水女子大学）教授．著書に『血液型と氣質』（三省堂）がある．）　*Eat Right for Your Type*『あなたの（血液）型にあったものを食べよう』

 _____ minutes _____ seconds

READING COMPREHENSION

Circle the letter of the best answer.

1. What is the passage mainly about?
   a. What blood does in our bodies.
   b. Important parts of our blood.
   c. Why blood types cannot be mixed.
   d. Three men who studied blood.

2. What did Karl Landsteiner discover?
   a. There are four types of personality.
   b. Blood is divided into four types.
   c. Blood type O is the most common.
   d. Blood from one person can be given to another.

3. According to the text, people with which blood type are most trustworthy?
   a. type A
   b. type B
   c. type AB
   d. type O

4. What kind of people are interested in Eat Right for Your Type?
   a. people who are too heavy
   b. people with type O blood
   c. Austrian people
   d. people who are worried about their blood

5. What is NOT true about blood type AB?
   a. It is the least common.
   b. It was discovered by Karl Landsteiner.
   c. People with this type are said to be original.
   d. People with this type lose weight easily.

LISTENING COMPREHENSION 27

Listen to the CD and fill in the blanks.

Karl Landsteiner (1)_____ a study in 1901 that showed there are four blood types. His study made it possible to be sure that people who need (2)_____ get the right type. His research helped save many lives. Many people now believe you can tell (3)_____ from blood type. For example, people with type B blood are said to be (4)_____, and those with type AB are said to be original. One book on blood types was a hit in America with people who want to (5)_____ weight.

VOCABULARY REINFORCEMENT

Circle the letter of the best answer.

1. Mike is so _____. He loves going to parties.
   a. outgoing
   b. curious
   c. generous
   d. honest

2. That artist's portraits are so _____.
   a. outgoing
   b. honest
   c. original
   d. generous

3. Helen is so _____. She loves giving people gifts.
   a. generous
   b. curious
   c. outgoing
   d. honest

4. You can't trust Clayton. He's just not _____.
   a. cruel
   b. honest
   c. original
   d. weak

5. Young children ask so many questions. They're really _____.
   a. generous
   b. original
   c. curious
   d. dangerous

IDIOMS

Find each idiom in the story and translate the sentences into Japanese.

1. (   ) (   ) (   ) = (興行などが) ヒットする
   This song has (   ) (   ) (   ) for a long time.

2. (   ) (   ) = 体重が減る, 痩せる
   She (   ) a lot of (   ) over the summer.（過去形で）

3. (   ) (   ) (something) = 〜を実行する
   The scientists (   ) (   ) an interesting study.（過去形で）

14 REALITY TV

リアリティー番組

　テレビ番組には，ドラマ・アニメ・音楽・バラエティ・スポーツ・ニュースなど様々な種類があります．あなたは，普段，どのような番組を見ていますか？　番組を見た翌日，友達と番組内容や出演した芸能人についてあれこれ話すのも楽しいですね．今回はリアリティー番組についてです．リアリティー番組と聞いて，どんな内容を想像しますか？

TARGET VOCABULARY

Look up each word in a dictionary and match it with the closest meaning.

1. define　　　_____ (　)
2. guide　　　_____ (　)
3. performer　_____ (　)
4. program　　_____ (　)
5. script　　　_____ (　)

a. someone who does something such as singing to entertain people
b. to give the meaning of
c. someone or something that leads; shows the way
d. a TV show
e. a written book or document with the words for actors to speak

READING PASSAGE

1   **Reality TV** shows are very popular. In fact, some **TV networks** only have reality shows! However, that does not mean all their **programs** are the same. There are many different kinds of reality shows.

   Some people **define** a reality TV show as one that has no **script**, but most
5 reality shows do use some kind of script to **guide** the show. The people on the show say and do things their own way. The script just lets them know what kinds of things will happen in the show.

   Probably the most well-known reality shows are talent shows. Each week the **performers** do something special and the people watching the show vote for
10 their favorite performance. *Star Search* (1980), *Top Chef* (2006), and *China's Got Talent* (2010) are examples of popular talent shows. There are also other types of reality shows such as game shows. These shows include programs like *Big Brother* (1999), *Survivor* (2000), and *Infinite Challenge* (2005).

   There are lots of other reality shows and these examples are just the tip of the
15 iceberg! Some reality TV shows focus on groups of people that help others. Some shows explain science and math in interesting ways. Others make history more interesting by showing families trying to live like people did in the past. There are even reality TV shows that help track down criminals.

224 words

Reality TV「リアリティー番組」(やらせや台本のない，素人の出演者による行動を放送する番組.) **TV networks**「テレビ放送網」 *Star Search*「スター・サーチ」(アメリカのタレント発掘番組.) *Top Chef*「トップ・シェフ」(アメリカの料理番組.) *China's Got Talent*「中国達人秀」(中国の公開オーディション番組.) *Big Brother*「ビッグ・ブラザー」(オランダのリアリティー番組.) *Survivor*「サバイバー」(サバイバル生活の番組.) *Infinite Challenge*「無限挑戦」(難題に挑戦する韓国の番組.)

READING COMPREHENSION

Circle the letter of the best answer.

1. What is the best title for the passage?
   a. Kinds of Reality TV Shows
   b. The First Reality TV Show
   c. Stars of Reality TV Shows
   d. The Most Popular Reality TV Show

2. What does the script of a reality TV show tell people?
   a. the show's TV schedule
   b. what to say on the show
   c. what guides on the show will do
   d. what will happen on the show

3. Which is the oldest reality TV game show mentioned in the passage?
   a. *Big Brother*
   b. *Survivor*
   c. *China's Got Talent*
   d. *Star Search*

4. Which of the following sentences is true about *Top Chef* and *Infinite Challenge*?
   a. Both shows were made before 2005.
   b. These shows are both talent shows.
   c. Neither show uses any kind of script.
   d. They are different kinds of reality shows.

5. What kind of reality TV show is NOT mentioned in the passage?
   a. one about groups that help people
   b. one for explaining science
   c. one about people falling in love
   d. one for tracking down criminals

LISTENING COMPREHENSION

Listen to the CD and fill in the blanks.

While some people might (1)_____ a reality show as one without a script, this is not always true. Many reality TV shows use scripts to (2)_____ the show without having to tell people what to say. Among the many kinds of reality TV programs broadcast today, some of the most popular are (3)_____ shows and game shows. But these are only the (4)_____ the iceberg for reality shows. Other kinds of reality shows focus on explaining things, showing people helping others, or even (5)_____ criminals.

55

VOCABULARY REINFORCEMENT

Circle the letter of the words that best match the words in *italics*.

1. Follow me. I can *take* you to the place you are looking for.
   a. explain
   b. perform
   c. define
   d. guide

2. We talked about many topics in class instead of *looking closely at* just one topic.
   a. caring for
   b. carrying out
   c. focusing on
   d. tracking down

3. I hope lots of people vote for this *person in the show*. I like the way he sings and dances.
   a. show
   b. chef
   c. performer
   d. script

4. Not many people watched the *show*, so the network stopped making it.
   a. criminal
   b. program
   c. record
   d. script

5. He left so many clues it was easy for the police to *find* the criminal.
   a. track down
   b. call
   c. define
   d. vote for

IDIOMS

Find each idiom in the story and translate the sentences into Japanese.

1. (   ) (   ) (   ) (   ) (   ) = 氷山の一角
   We learned about two of da Vinci's inventions, but those are only (   ) (   ) (   ) (   ) (   ).

2. (   ) (   ) = 〜に焦点を合わせる，〜に重点的に取り組む
   We have a lot of information to study for the history test, so today let us just (   ) (   ) important dates.

3. (   ) (   ) = 〜を見つけ出す，〜を追い詰める
   Using their noses, the dogs (   ) (   ) the fox.（過去形で）

15 RODEOS
ロデオ

写真を見て，何をしているところかわかりますか？ これはロデオといって，荒馬を乗りこなす技術を競うスポーツです．かつては，カウボーイの仲間内での腕自慢の遊びでしたが，現在では，プロスポーツとして大会が開催されています．さあ，ロデオについて読んでみましょう．

TARGET VOCABULARY

Look up each word in a dictionary and match it with the closest meaning.

1. cowboy　_____　(　)　a. an important happening; a competition or contest
2. saddle　_____　(　)　b. to join something together with a rope or string
3. wrestle　_____　(　)　c. a man who works with horses and cows
4. tie　_____　(　)　d. a seat on a horse's back
5. event　_____　(　)　e. to fight by throwing down and holding someone

57

READING PASSAGE

1   The word *rodeo* comes from the Spanish word *rodear*, meaning surround, used to describe a place where **cowboys** sold **cows**.

   In the 1800s, cowboys from all over the southwestern United States came together a few times each year in order to sell their cows. After selling the cows, the cowboys often took part in **competitions** where they showed off the skills they had learned over the past year. In 1888, the people of **Prescott**, Arizona, began to sell tickets to these cowboy shows, and prizes were given to the best cowboy acts.

   Since the original rodeo in 1888, the popularity of rodeos has grown. Now people can see them all year round in parts of North America and Australia. There are even rodeo competitions in Korea and Japan. For the cowboys who compete in the rodeos, they can get more than just a chance to show off skills. They can win a lot of money. For that reason, some people choose to become professional rodeo cowboys instead of professional **ranch** cowboys. Cowboys in the rodeo finals today can win millions of dollars.

   The most popular **events** to see at rodeos are **bull wrestling**, catching and **tying calves**, and wild horse riding, which is done with and without a **saddle**.

   In bull wrestling, the cowboy must jump onto the back of a running bull. Using only his hands, the cowboy gets the bull to stop by making it fall to the ground. The cowboy who can do this the fastest is the winner.

                                                                                               252 words

   cows「雌牛, 乳牛」 Prescott「プレスコット」(アリゾナ州中部の都市. 夏に Frontier Days Rodeo が開催される.) competition「競技, コンテスト」 ranch「牧場」 bull「雄牛」 calf「子牛」

   _____ minutes _____ seconds

READING COMPREHENSION

Circle the letter of the best answer.

1. The passage is about . . .
   a. the events in a rodeo.
   b. the origin and popularity of rodeos.
   c. the spread of rodeos to other countries.
   d. all of the above.

2. In which country was the first rodeo held?
   a. Spain
   b. the United States
   c. Korea
   d. Japan

3. How often are rodeos held today in the United States?
   a. a few times a year
   b. many times throughout the year
   c. every few years
   d. The article does not say.

4. According to the passage, why do some people become rodeo cowboys?
   a. to travel in North America
   b. to become ranch cowboys
   c. to win money
   d. to find good saddles

5. What does a cowboy NOT have to do in bull wrestling?
   a. get a bull to fall to the ground
   b. jump onto the back of a bull
   c. compete quickly
   d. use a rope

LISTENING COMPREHENSION 31

Listen to the CD and fill in the blanks.

A long time ago, cowboys (1)_____ once a year to sell cows. After all the cows were sold, the cowboys had free time, so they often (2)_____ their skills to each other. In 1888, one town started selling (3)_____ to these shows. During these shows today, cowboys compete in various (4)_____. These include riding horses, (5)_____ bulls, and tying calves.

59

VOCABULARY REINFORCEMENT

Circle the letter of the word or phrase that best completes the sentence.

1. Be careful! There is a dangerous _____ in that field.
   a. saddle
   b. bull
   c. cowboy
   d. event

2. The mountain climber died because she did not _____ her rope correctly.
   a. tie
   b. wrestle
   c. murder
   d. come together

3. I traveled _____ Europe when I was young.
   a. on the go
   b. long ago
   c. all over
   d. all year round

4. Jenny loves horse riding, so her parents bought her _____ for her birthday.
   a. a bull
   b. a saddle
   c. an event
   d. a calf

5. Sam loves _____ his expensive car.
   a. attempting
   b. wrestling
   c. concerning
   d. showing off

IDIOMS

Find each idiom in the story and translate the sentences into Japanese.

1. (   ) (   ) (   ) = 一年中
   In Singapore, it's hot (   ) (   ) (   ).

2. (   ) (   ) = (能力などを) 誇示する
   The company (   ) (   ) their new product at the mall.（過去形で）

3. (   ) (   ) = ～の至るところで
   There are Chinese restaurants (   ) (   ) the world.

60

16　WOMEN'S SUMO

女子相撲

　日本の国技といえば，相撲ですね．まげを結った大男が力の限りぶつかり合う一番は迫力満点です．昔は小学生の男の子たちが人気力士をまねして砂場で相撲を取る光景がよく見られました．しかし，今は相撲を取るのは男性だけではありません．写真のように女子相撲の大会が開催されています．あなたは女子相撲のどういう点が興味深いですか？

TARGET VOCABULARY

Look up each word in a dictionary and match it with the closest meaning.

1. prize　　　　　_____ ( )　a. a person who plays or does a sport
2. athlete　　　　_____ ( )　b. important; one of the largest
3. compete　　　 _____ ( )　c. to play or do a sport in order to win
4. international　 _____ ( )　d. among or between two or more countries
5. major　　　　 _____ ( )　e. something a person wins

READING PASSAGE

1   Sumo, the type of wrestling found in Japan, has a problem. It may have to let go of some past traditions in order to become a **major international** sport, and one of the biggest changes may be allowing women to **compete**.

   Traditionally, women cannot enter a sumo ring. That caused a problem for the female **governor of Osaka**. She could not enter the ring to give **prizes** to the winners of a big sumo competition in Osaka. In the end, her male assistant had to hand out the prizes.

   The governor of Osaka only wanted to stand in the ring to hand out prizes. Other women want to enter the sumo ring to compete! Some people think this would be a good thing for sumo. There is a rule that all sports in the Olympics must be open to men and women. **Unless** sumo opens the ring to women, it will never become an Olympic sport.

   Sumo has already spread from Japan to other countries. In fact, since the 1990s, women's sumo has been growing in popularity in Europe. Female **athletes** from Europe seem to be quite good at sumo! This has **led to** another problem. Female athletes from outside Japan are winning more sumo competitions than female athletes from Japan! At an international competition in Warsaw, Poland, only one Japanese athlete won a medal. All the other medals went to women who were not from Japan.

237 words

Notes

governor of Osaka「大阪府知事」　**unless**「～しない限り」　**lead to**「～を引き起こす，～の原因となる」

_____ minutes _____ seconds

READING COMPREHENSION

Circle the letter of the best answer.

1. This reading is about . . .
   a. a female athlete who has won many prizes.
   b. how a sport is changing.
   c. a new sport for young people in Japan.
   d. the rules of an international sport.

2. Which of the following is true about the governor of Osaka?
   a. She enjoys women's sumo wrestling.
   b. She was a sumo athlete.
   c. She made a new rule about sumo rings.
   d. She did not hand out prizes after a competition.

3. How would sumo benefit by allowing women to compete in Japan?
   a. Different kinds of sumo rings could be made.
   b. More people would watch competitions.
   c. Male athletes would not need to be as big.
   d. The sport would meet one of the Olympic rules.

4. Where is sumo wrestling growing in popularity?
   a. Europe
   b. Poland
   c. Japan
   d. The United States

5. How many Japanese sumo wrestlers won medals at the Warsaw competition mentioned in the passage?
   a. none
   b. one
   c. three
   d. all of them

LISTENING COMPREHENSION 33

Listen to the CD and fill in the blanks.

The sport of sumo wrestling may need to (1)_____ some of its traditions. In order to become an Olympic sport, female (2)_____ must be allowed to compete in the sport. This might be difficult. Traditionally, women cannot even step in a sumo ring. In fact, the governor of Osaka could not (3) _____ prizes after a major competition. Her male (4)_____ had to do it. Women's sumo may not be popular in Japan, but that is not true in other places. As an (5)_____ sport, women's sumo has been growing in popularity in Europe.

VOCABULARY REINFORCEMENT

Circle the letter of the word or phrase that best matches the word(s) in *italics*.

1. The final exam is an *important* part of your grade in this class.
   a. dangerous
   b. international
   c. major
   d. terrible

2. Animals like snakes have to take off their *body covering* in order to grow larger.
   a. governor
   b. history
   c. prize
   d. skin

3. Here are ten free tickets to the concert. You can *give them away* to your friends.
   a. get in them
   b. grow in popularity
   c. hand them out
   d. let go of them

4. I have too much work to do. I need a *helper*.
   a. assistant
   b. athlete
   c. owner
   d. researcher

5. My brother *takes part in* the city tennis tournament every year.
   a. avoids
   b. competes
   c. shouts
   d. traps

IDIOMS

Find each idiom in the story and translate the sentences into Japanese.

1. (　　　) (　　　) (　　　) = 〜を取り除く，〜をやめる
   In order to make new friends in the small town, he had to (　　　) (　　　) (　　　) many of his "big city" ways.

2. (　　　) (　　　) = 配る
   The teacher will (　　　) (　　　) the test after everyone sits down.

3. (　　　) (　　　) (　　　) = 人気が出る
   The singer (　　　) (　　　) (　　　) after one of her songs was used on a television show.（過去形で）

17 STUDYING ABROAD

外国で学ぼう

あなたは留学したことがありますか？ または，留学経験を持つ家族・親戚・友達がいますか？ 留学先の国はどこでしたか？ 人気のある留学先はどこの国だと思いますか？ その国の言葉で授業を受けたり，現地の人とコミュニケーションを取ったりすることで語学力が向上します．異文化を受け入れることを学ぶのも非常に重要ですね．

TARGET VOCABULARY

Look up each word in a dictionary and match it with the closest meaning.

1. require　　＿＿＿＿＿（ ）　a. finish school or university
2. fee　　　　＿＿＿＿＿（ ）　b. ask for admission or acceptance
3. apply　　　＿＿＿＿＿（ ）　c. a cost
4. graduate　 ＿＿＿＿＿（ ）　d. go into; begin
5. enter　　　＿＿＿＿＿（ ）　e. need

READING PASSAGE

1   Every year, thousands of students travel to foreign countries to study. More than 30 percent of these students go to the United States, the United Kingdom, or Australia. France and Germany are also popular countries with **international students**. In fact, almost half of all international students can be found in these five countries.

No matter where a student chooses to study, there are some things universities around the world **require**. First, all students must **graduate** from high school before they can **apply** to a university. Most universities also require some kind of test for students to **enter** the university. Universities in the United States, Australia, and Canada usually require some kind of **standardized exam**, such as the **SAT**. Students who do not come from **English-speaking countries** also must take a test such as the **TOEFL** or the **IELTS** to show they know enough English to study in English.

In most countries, students must apply to each university they hope to go to. However, students applying to universities in the United Kingdom can use one form to apply to several universities at the same time. Students can apply to five courses at one time with one **UCAS** application. This can save students a lot of time and money.

For universities in other countries, students must fill out different forms for each university and pay a **fee** with each application.

Many governments are trying to increase the number of international students studying in their countries. International students spend around AU$6 billion in Australia each year.

253 words

Notes

international student「留学生」　**standardized exam**「標準化テスト」（試験時間，問題数，回答方法などの測定方法と基準を確立したテスト．）　**English-speaking countries**「英語圏」　**SAT**「進学適性試験」（アメリカの高校生が4年制大学に進学するときに受験する全国共通試験．）　**TOEFL**「トフル」（主としてアメリカやカナダへの留学を希望する，英語を母語としない学生を対象とした英語のテスト．）　**IELTS**「アイエルツ」（主としてイギリス，オーストラリアへの留学を希望する，英語を母語としない学生を対象とした英語のテスト．）　**UCAS**（イギリスの大学へ入学するための出願申請機関．）

 _____ minutes _____ seconds

READING COMPREHENSION

Circle the letter of the best answer.

1. This reading is about . . .
   a. how to do well when studying abroad.
   c. what is required to study abroad.
   b. the best country for studying abroad.
   d. why students study abroad.

2. Which of the following is NOT one of the top five locations for students studying abroad?
   a. Australia
   c. the United Kingdom
   b. Canada
   d. the United States

3. Most universities in Australia . . .
   a. require students to take a standardized test.
   b. accept students who have not graduated from high school.
   c. have no fees for applying.
   d. require the TOEFL test.

4. What is different about applying to universities in the United Kingdom?
   a. You need to take the SAT exam.
   c. The fees are more expensive.
   b. The universities reply faster.
   d. You can use one form for many schools.

5. Which of these requirements is NOT discussed in the passage?
   a. fees
   c. tests
   b. graduating from high school
   d. language classes

LISTENING COMPREHENSION 35

Listen to the CD and fill in the blanks.

Here are a few tips for students who want to study abroad. First, (1)_____ where you want to study, you have to (2)_____ from high school. Then, of course, you have to fill out the right forms and pay the (3)_____ to apply to each university. Many universities also need students to take tests before they can (4)_____ the university.

VOCABULARY REINFORCEMENT

Circle the letter of the best answer.

1. Before you can _____ the theater, you must give the man your ticket.
   a. afford
   b. choose
   c. enter
   d. require

2. She _____ from college with the highest grade in her class.
   a. applied
   b. graduated
   c. entered
   d. prepared

3. He made a mistake when he was _____ the credit card application.
   a. training for
   b. filling out
   c. saving time
   d. telling apart

4. We both _____ to the art school, but my friend did not get in.
   a. applied
   b. entered
   c. graduated
   d. connected

5. Can you tell me which _____ I should fill out to apply for a visa?
   a. role
   b. fee
   c. form
   d. band

IDIOMS

Find each idiom in the story and translate the sentences into Japanese.

1. (   ) (   ) (what, where, who, etc.) = たとえ（何を、どこで、誰が）しようとも
   He will not change his mind (   ) (   ) what you say.

2. (   ) (   ) = （用紙などに）記入する
   Please (   ) (   ) this form and then give it back to me.

3. (   ) (   ) = （時間を）節約する
   If we go down Main Street, we can (   ) (   ).

18 THE PALACE OF SALT

しょっぱいホテル

　ホテルに宿泊したことがありますか？ そのなかで一番思い出深い場所はどこですか？ 日本にはペットと一緒に泊まることができるホテルがありますが，世界にはもっと変わったホテルが数多くあります．今回の話はしょっぱいホテルです．しょっぱいと聞いて，どんなホテルだと思いますか？

TARGET VOCABULARY

Look up each word in a dictionary and match it with the closest meaning.

1. palace　　　_____ ( )　a. tables, chairs, beds, etc.
2. cave　　　　_____ ( )　b. not exist anymore; vanish
3. furniture　　_____ ( )　c. a rectangular piece of something
4. block　　　 _____ ( )　d. hole in a mountain
5. disappear　 _____ ( )　e. a very large house; place where a king or queen lives

READING PASSAGE

1   There are many unique hotels around the world. In Sweden, you can stay in a hotel made out of ice, open between December and April every year. In Turkey, you can stay in a **cave** hotel with a television and a bathroom in each room. And in Bolivia, you can stay at the *Palacio de Sal* (**Palace** of Salt).

5   Thousands of years ago, the area around the Palace of Salt was a large lake. But over time, all the water **disappeared**. Today, the area has only two small lakes and two **salt deserts**.

The larger of the two deserts, **the Uyuni salt desert**, is 12,000 square kilometers. During the day, the desert is bright white because of the salt. There
10 are no roads across the Uyuni desert, so local people must show guests the way to the hotel.

In the early 1990s, a man named Juan Quesada cut big **blocks** of salt from the desert. He used the blocks to build the hotel. Everything in the hotel is made out of salt: the walls, the roof, even the **furniture**, so the tables, the chairs, the beds,
15 and the hotel's bar are all made of salt.

The sun heats the walls and roof during the day. At night the desert is very cold, but the rooms stay warm. The hotel has sixteen rooms. A single room costs about $100 a night, and a double room costs about $130.

A sign on the hotel's wall tells guests, "Please do not lick the walls."

251 words

Notes

salt deserts「塩湖」(塩湖とは，大昔に海水が陸地に閉じ込められてできた湖で，その湖の水分が蒸発して塩分が残ったもの.)　the Uyuni salt desert「ウユニ塩湖」(ボリビア南西部のアンデス高地の標高約 3,700 メートルにある.)

_____ minutes _____ seconds

READING COMPREHENSION

Circle the letter of the best answer.

1. What is unique about the Salt Palace Hotel?
   a. its long history
   b. the price of the rooms
   c. the guests that stay there
   d. what it is made of

2. Which sentence about the area around the Palace of Salt is NOT true?
   a. It was a lake many years ago.
   b. It is white during the day.
   c. There are several roads to the hotel.
   d. It is more than 10,000 square kilometers.

3. Where did the salt used for the hotel come from?
   a. a salt factory
   b. the ground
   c. Turkey
   d. the walls of the hotel

4. Who is Juan Quesada?
   a. a hotel guest
   b. a guide
   c. the hotel's owner
   d. an expert on salt

5. What keeps the rooms warm at night?
   a. heat from the walls
   b. the desert air
   c. the sun
   d. the furniture

LISTENING COMPREHENSION

Listen to the CD and fill in the blanks.

In Bolivia, there is a unique hotel made of salt. The English name of the hotel is the (1)_____ of Salt. The hotel is in the middle of a salt (2)_____. One man had the idea to make a hotel there. The hotel is unique because the walls are (3)_____ salt. The man cut big (4)_____ of salt from the floor of the desert. He used the blocks to make the walls, the roof, and the (5)_____ for the hotel.

VOCABULARY REINFORCEMENT

Circle the letter of the words that best match the words in *italics*.

1. The bear found a *cave* in the side of the mountain and slept there during the winter.
   a. cage
   b. hole
   c. desert
   d. surface

2. I know where this office is. Let me *show you the way*.
   a. connect you
   b. guide you
   c. shout at you
   d. disappear from you

3. The *palace* is only open for tours between 10 a.m. and 5 p.m.
   a. bell tower
   b. bird's nest
   c. gum's taste
   d. king's home

4. I also need to get some new *chairs and tables* for the living room.
   a. blocks
   b. stones
   c. furniture
   d. marble

5. This plant is found only in *deserts*.
   a. forests
   b. caves
   c. dry areas
   d. zoos

IDIOMS

Find each idiom in the story and translate the sentences into Japanese.

1. (   ) (   ) (   ) = (〜への) 道を教える，連れて行く
   Excuse me. Could you please (   ) (   ) (   ) to my room?

2. (   ) (   ) = 時がたてば，(過去のことについて) やがて
   The problem will get worse (   ) (   ) if we don't do something about it.

3. (   ) (   ) (   ) = 〜 (材料) から作られる
   The house in the forest was (   ) (   ) (   ) pine logs.

19 THE MONA LISA

モナリザの微笑

　こちらを向いて優しく微笑む美女，そう今回はみなさんご存じのモナリザの話です．現在，パリのルーブル美術館で展示されているモナリザですが，いつ頃，誰によって描かれたのでしょうか？　実はモナリザは，100年以上前に大変な目に遭っています．はたしてどんなことが起きたのでしょうか？

TARGET VOCABULARY

Look up each word in a dictionary and match it with the closest meaning.

1. portrait　　_____ ( )
2. museum　　_____ ( )
3. visitor　　_____ ( )
4. hide　　_____ ( )
5. steal　　_____ ( )

a. to take something from someone without asking
b. a painting of a person
c. to put something where people can't find it
d. a place that show valuable art or historical objects
e. a tourist

73

READING PASSAGE

1   **Leonardo da Vinci** began painting **the Mona Lisa**, one of the most famous paintings of all time, in 1503. He was working on a special painting for a church at the time, but it was not going well. The woman who can be seen in the Mona Lisa is said to be Madonna Lisa del Giocondo. She was the wife of an Italian
5 businessman who asked da Vinci to paint a **portrait** of her.

   After da Vinci finished the painting in 1506 he was invited by the French King, **Francois I**, to visit France, and he took the painting with him. Today the Mona Lisa is kept in **the Louvre**, an art **museum** in Paris, and it is seen by about six million **visitors** a year.

10   The painting measures only 77 centimeters by 53 centimeters and is painted with oil on wood. In 1911, it was **stolen** by a worker at the Louvre, Vincenzo Peruggia, who took it out of the museum by **hiding** it under his coat. Two years later police found the painting under Peruggia's bed after he tried to sell it.

   In 1962, the Mona Lisa was taken to Washington and New York for an
15 **exhibition**. For the journey, it was insured for 100 million dollars, making it the most valuable painting ever!

216 words

Notes

Leonardo da Vinci「レオナルド・ダ・ビンチ」(イタリアの画家・建築家・音楽家・数学者・科学者.) **the Mona Lisa**「モナリザ」(レオナルド・ダ・ビンチ作の婦人肖像画.) **Francois I**「フランソワ一世」 **the Louvre**「ルーブル美術館」(1793年にフランスによって設立された. そのコレクションは絵画を含む7つの部門に分かれている.) **exhibition**「展覧会」

 _____ minutes _____ seconds

READING COMPREHENSION

Circle the letter of the best answer.

1. What is the best title for this passage?
    a. Leonardo da Vinci—an Interesting Painter
    b. The Louvre—a Famous French Art Museum
    c. Vincenzo Peruggia—the Man Who Stole the Mona Lisa
    d. The Mona Lisa—the Most Valuable Painting of All Time

2. When did Leonardo da Vinci finish painting the Mona Lisa?
    a. 1503
    b. 1506
    c. 1911
    d. 1962

3. Who is Madonna Lisa del Giocondo said to be?
    a. the painter of the Mona Lisa
    b. the woman in the painting
    c. the wife of the French king
    d. the woman who asked da Vinci to paint the Mona Lisa.

4. Why did da Vinci go to France?
    a. to visit the Louvre
    b. to paint the Mona Lisa
    c. He was invited by Francois I.
    d. He was invited by Madonna Lisa del Giocondo.

5. What sentence about Vincenzo Peruggia is NOT true?
    a. He worked in an art museum.
    b. He stole the Mona Lisa.
    c. He sold the painting.
    d. He hid the painting under his bed.

LISTENING COMPREHENSION 39

Listen to the CD and fill in the blanks.

The Mona Lisa, a portrait (1) _____ of a woman called Madonna Lisa del Giocondo, is the most famous painting of all time. Six million (2)_____ see it every year. It was (3)_____ in 1911, but the police found it hidden under a museum worker's bed.

VOCABULARY REINFORCEMENT

Circle the letter of the best answer.

1. Be careful with this glass. It's really _____.
   - a. intelligent
   - b. fee
   - c. valuable
   - d. insured

2. That's a great _____ of Kimberley. It looks just like her.
   - a. program
   - b. desert
   - c. exhibition
   - d. portrait

3. The race _____ for Rupert. He won!
   - a. went well
   - b. expanded
   - c. matched
   - d. stole

4. New York is famous for its _____.
   - a. visitors
   - b. museums
   - c. caves
   - d. palaces

5. My new bicycle was _____ in front of my house.
   - a. hidden
   - b. disappeared
   - c. stolen
   - d. invited

IDIOMS

Find each idiom in the story and translate the sentences into Japanese.

1. (   ) (   ) (   ) = 〜であると言われている
   Prudle the parrot (   ) (   ) (   ) know over 800 English words. （過去形で）

2. (   ) (   ) = うまくいく
   Rebecca's new job is (   ) really (   ). She's very happy. （進行形で）

3. (   ) (   ) (   ) = これまでで，史上
   The tallest man (   ) (   ) (   ) was 2.72 meters tall.

20 LIZARDS

トカゲは好きですか

あなたはトカゲを触ったり，抱いたりすることができますか？ トカゲを気持悪いと思う人がいる一方で，トカゲが大好きでペットにする人たちもいます．トカゲはよいペットになると思いますか？ トカゲを飼うことは簡単なのでしょうか，それとも難しいのでしょうか？

TARGET VOCABULARY

Look up each word in a dictionary and match it with the closest meaning.

1. active　　　_____ (　)　a. to cause pain
2. during　　 _____ (　)　b. awake and moving around; busy
3. hurt　　　 _____ (　)　c. to hurt or damage by moving something
4. noise　　　_____ (　)　　　sharp across the surface
5. scratch　　_____ (　)　d. something you hear; sound
　　　　　　　　　　　　　　　　e. at the time of

READING PASSAGE

1   **Lizards** are unusual, but they can make good pets because most of them are small and easy to care for. They do not make loud **noises**, and they do not need to go for walks or take baths.

　　Of course, some lizards make better pets than others. One of the most popular
5 lizards in pet stores is the **bearded dragon**. Bearded dragons are active **during** the day and do not mind people holding them. **Geckos** are another popular pet lizard. They are a little more difficult to care for. Geckos are **active** at night and need a warm place to live. Like bearded dragons, they can be held by their owners. Both of these lizards can live ten years or more when they are well
10 cared for.

　　Two lizards that are bad choices for pets are **iguanas** and **chameleons**. Iguanas can grow to be almost two meters (nearly six **feet**), so they need a big space to live in. They can also bite or **scratch** their owners. Chameleons do not **hurt** their owners, but they are quite difficult to care for. While iguanas can live
15 up to twenty years, chameleons do not live very long. Most do not live more than five years.

203 words

Notes

lizard「トカゲ」　bearded dragon「フトアゴヒゲトカゲ」(トカゲの一種.)　gecko「ヤモリ」　iguana「イグアナ」　chameleon「カメレオン」　feet「フィート」(1 フィートは 30.48 センチ.)

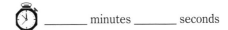
_____ minutes _____ seconds

READING COMPREHENSION

Circle the letter of the best answer.

1. This reading is about . . .
    a. good and bad pets.
    b. how to tell male from female lizards.
    c. why lizards are disappearing.
    d. wild animals.

2. What is true according to the passage?
    a. It is not hard to care for most lizards.
    b. Lizards are better than dogs or cats.
    c. Lizard bites can be dangerous.
    d. Pet lizards need walks and baths.

3. Which lizard would be good for a child to watch and play with during the day?
    a. a bearded dragon
    b. a chameleon
    c. a gecko
    d. an iguana

4. Which lizard lives the longest?
    a. a bearded dragon
    b. a chameleon
    c. a gecko
    d. an iguana

5. What would the writer of the passage probably say is true?
    a. Iguanas are not good pets for children.
    b. It is more difficult to care for a gecko than for a chameleon.
    c. Most lizards are dangerous, so do not keep them as pets.
    d. No matter which lizard you get, do not hold it.

LISTENING COMPREHENSION   41

Listen to the CD and fill in the blanks.

Lizards are good pets because they are actually easy to (1)_____. Lizards do not need to go for walks or take baths like dogs. They also do not usually hurt their owners by biting or (2)_____ them like cats. Lizards are also good pets to keep in apartments because they do not make any (3)_____ so they will not bother neighbors. One kind of lizard called a bearded dragon is popular these days. It is (4)_____ during the day and does not mind being held. It will not (5)_____ people. So it is a good pet for kids!

VOCABULARY REINFORCEMENT

Circle the letter of the word or phrase that best completes the sentence.

1. The dog _____ its ear with one of its back legs.
   a. disappeared
   b. entered
   c. required
   d. scratched

2. He was surprised by the loud _____ from the other room.
   a. cave
   b. desert
   c. form
   d. noise

3. The fish were very _____. They were swimming all around the tank.
   a. active
   b. bearded
   c. international
   d. major

4. My father _____ cutting the grass in our yard. In fact, I think he enjoys it.
   a. cares for
   b. does not mind
   c. shows the way
   d. takes a bath

5. Several people left the theater _____ the movie.
   a. as for
   b. during
   c. instead of
   d. while

IDIOMS

Find each idiom in the story and translate the sentences into Japanese.

1. (   ) (   ) = ～の世話をする
   We found a hungry baby bird on the ground, so we took it home and (   ) (   ) it.（過去形で）

2. (   ) (   ) (   ) = 入浴する，風呂につかる
   The last time she (   ) (   ) (   ) was several months ago. Usually she takes a shower.（過去形で）

3. (   ) (   ) (   ) = ～を気にしない，何とも思わない
   His cat (   ) (   ) (   ) staying at home all day alone.（過去形で）

Word Per Minute (WPM) 記録シート

時間を計りながら全体の内容を短時間で読み取る速読をしてみましょう．本文の最後に単語数が掲載されています．読み終えたら，単語数を読了時間で割ります．例えば，200語の文を4分で読み終えた場合，200語（単語数）÷ 4分（読了時間）＝分速50語（WPM）です．毎回，WPMを記録しておけば，速読力の伸びがわかります．

Unit	単語数	読了時間	WPM			50		100		150		200
記入例	200	4:00	50.0			●						
Unit 1	213	:										
Unit 2	240	:										
Unit 3	204	:										
Unit 4	227	:										
Unit 5	206	:										
Unit 6	207	:										
Unit 7	205	:										
Unit 8	205	:										
Unit 9	237	:										
Unit 10	207	:										
Unit 11	248	:										
Unit 12	250	:										
Unit 13	253	:										
Unit 14	224	:										
Unit 15	252	:										
Unit 16	237	:										
Unit 17	253	:										
Unit 18	251	:										
Unit 19	216	:										
Unit 20	203	:										

TEXT PRODUCTION STAFF

edited by
Eiichi Kanno

編集
菅野 英一

English-language editing by
Bill Benfield

英文校閲
ビル・ベンフィールド

cover design by
Fumio Takahashi (AZ)

表紙デザイン
高橋文雄（AZ）

CD PRODUCTION STAFF

recorded by
Erika Wiseberg (AmE)
Chris Wells (AmE)

吹き込み者
エリカ・ワイズバーグ（アメリカ英語）
クリス・ウェルズ（アメリカ英語）

Basic Faster Reading —New Edition—
速読の基礎演習―最新版―

2015年1月20日　初版　発行
2025年4月5日　第6刷　発行

著　者　Casey Malarcher
　　　　原田 慎一

発行者　佐野 英一郎

発行所　株式会社 成美堂
　　　　〒101-0052　東京都千代田区神田小川町3-22
　　　　TEL 03-3291-2261　FAX 03-3293-5490
　　　　https://www.seibido.co.jp

印刷・製本　三美印刷（株）

ISBN 978-4-7919-3381-5　　　　　　　　　　　Printed in Japan

・落丁・乱丁本はお取り替えします。
・本書の無断複写は、著作権上の例外を除き著作権侵害となります。